JOEY
DUNLOP
KING OF THE ROADS

Stephen Davison with Joey Dunlop during the TT 2000 prize presentation.

STEPHEN DAVISON was born in 1961 and is a native of Tardree, County Antrim. A graduate in History from Queen's University, Belfast, he has been a photographer since 1990 and a staff photographer with the Belfast photographic agency Pacemaker Press International since 1994. He has been a fan of Joey Dunlop since first seeing him race in 1975 and it was seeing the pictures of Joey's achievements in motorcycle publications that inspired him to pick up a camera. Now living in Kells, County Antrim, Davison has won various photographic awards, including the Northern Ireland Sports Photographer and Northern Ireland Press Photographer titles.

JOEY DUNLOP
KING OF THE ROADS

Photographs and text by

STEPHEN DAVISON

THE O'BRIEN PRESS
DUBLIN

PACEMAKER PRESS INTERNATIONAL
BELFAST

First published 2000 by The O'Brien Press Ltd,
20 Victoria Road, Dublin 6, Ireland.
Tel. +353 1 4923333; Fax. +353 1 4922777
E-mail books@obrien.ie
Website www.obrien.ie

ISBN: 0-86278-698-3

British Library Cataloguing-in-Publication Data
A catalogue record for this title is available from the British Library

2 3 4 5 6 7 8 9 10
00 01 02 03 04 05 06 07

The O'Brien Press receives
assistance from

The Arts Council
An Chomhairle Ealaíon

Editing, typesetting, layout, design: The O'Brien Press Ltd.
Cover design: Mark J Cairnes
Layout and design: Designit
Photographs: Pacemaker Press International, Belfast
Printing: Zure S.A.

Contents

Acknowledgements

I would like to offer my sincerest thanks to the following people for their help with this book:
To the Dunlop family for their help and understanding during the hardest of times. In particular, I am extremely grateful to Linda Dunlop for her assistance and support.

To Martin Wright, the proprietor of Pacemaker Press International (i.e., the boss!), for his determination to make this book happen. Also to my colleagues, David, Stephen and William, for keeping my share of the work covered when I was working on the book.

To Michael O'Brien and the staff at the O'Brien Press, especially to the Belfast wing of O'Brien Press, namely Damian Keenan, for his initial belief in the idea, and Rachel Pierce, whose patience and forbearance during the editing stages has been put to the severest of tests.

To Jackie Fullerton and Rod Nawn who have given invaluable help in providing the introduction at very short notice.

To Clifford McClean and Gavan Caldwell, whose dedication in sourcing the early pictures for this project knew no bounds.

To Leslie Moore of *Road Racing Ireland*, John Savage of the *Newtownards Chronicle* and Paul Lindsay of *Irish Racer* for allowing me to avail of their encyclopaedic knowledge of motorcycle road racing. I could not have written the captions without them.

To designers Mark Cairns and Frank Murphy, who coped brilliantly with having such a mammoth task thrust upon them at very short notice.

To my wife Hazel and our girls, Emma and Laura, for putting up with Dad not being around very much over the past few months. Sorry.

And finally to my uncles, Johnny, Sandy and Samuel James, for handing down their love of motorcycles and road racing. I hope I have not let you down.

Stephen Davison

Pal Joey / The King

*'Now you've set this incredible record, any thoughts of retirement?'
I asked him. 'I always said I'd only retire when you did, Jackie!'
came the laughing response.*

Joey Dunlop was just back from the Isle of Man, sitting in his own packed Ballymoney pub, celebrating with friends his incredible achievements of the previous week. He had just completed a fantastic TT hat-trick on 'the Island', and at forty-eight years of age was not merely defying the years but relishing them – in and out of the saddle.

I was privileged to have known, admired and befriended the greatest road racing motorcyclist of all time. I called him 'The King', which both amused and bemused him. He knew he was good – he couldn't have set the records he did if he believed otherwise. But Joey Dunlop did not need to tell anyone what he knew: that he was the best.

A singular man, his satisfaction came from proving his mastery of machines and roads and applying his huge talent to the goals he set himself throughout his life. From his early days in and around the small north Antrim village of Armoy, through the learning curves of Kirkistown and Dundrod in the 1970s, and during the

In the early 1970s, Joey was one of a group of north Antrim racers who became known as the 'Armoy Armada'. Sharing this title were Frank Kennedy, Jim Dunlop, Joey's brother, and his brother-in-law, Mervyn Robinson. Throughout the decade they did battle with the 'Dromara Destroyers' – Raymond McCullough, Trevor Steele and Brian Reid from County Down. Sadly, Jim Dunlop is the only surviving member of the 'Armada'.

Formula One world championship triumphs of the 1980s, Joey Dunlop was always setting new targets, drawing new horizons.

Joey is flanked by John Rea and his wife, Bessie, as he sits on the Yamsel 350cc that the Rea brothers bought for him in 1976. John Rea was one of the first sponsors to realise Joey's potential and along with his brothers, Noel and Martin, began to support Joey by providing him with competitive machinery. The association between the Rea family and the Dunlops continued with both of Joey's brothers, Jim and Robert, racing this same Yamsel bike in later years.

To use clichés when talking about Joey is to do this most modest and thoughtful of men a disservice. Nonetheless, he was a 'one-off' – a true legend of motor sport. Ask Carl Fogarty, Steve Hislop, Ron Haslam, Giacomo Agostini or that other great Ulster racer, Philip McCallen, and as one voice they'll acclaim him as the rider of this and every generation. In spite of this, Joey never tried to adapt to the often superficial demands of the sport's PR machinery. He was a superstar, but he would not learn that particular script! There would always be a loose nut to tighten, a petrol tank cap to find in the haven of his workshop or a bike needing repair that would command his attention – leaving no room for the vanities of a superstar lifestyle. Apart from the quiet and loving warmth he found in his family, it was around his bikes that Joey was most at ease. The honours may have piled up, many champagne bottles may have been cracked open in victory celebrations, there may have been visits with royalty to pick up well-merited 'gongs' for his services to his sporting passion and for his unstinting charity work, but above and beyond it all, Joey Dunlop was a biker.

Joey takes a break with his brother-in-law, Mervyn Robinson, during practice for the Ulster Grand Prix in 1975. Neighbours in the County Antrim village of Armoy, Joey followed Mervyn into racing and they became intense rivals as well as close friends.

Joey enjoyed a drink, and we whiled away many a night over a glass. In the modern jargon he was 'focussed' as no one else was as far as racing was concerned. When he turned those eyes on you – those eyes that fixed the road ahead so firmly – they gave a clear signal if your approach would be welcomed or rebuffed! But in relaxed conversation he was a delightful and marvellously informed companion.

Linda, his wife, and his lovely children understood that his instincts guided him, and neither he nor they ever had cause for regret. Their dad

But his intelligence wasn't confined to handling a 750cc Superbike, though that is where it shone most obviously and brightly. He was also well travelled. He went to the newly created nations after the break-up of the Soviet Union, sometimes at the drop of a hat, and often alone, and became expert on Eastern European social and sporting cultures.

Alongside his passion for racing, his charity work was all-important to him. The adulation he enjoyed – but never quite understood – over his three decades of racing supremacy stretched from mid-Antrim to Malaysia, from the Temple to Tokyo. But one always suspected that the smiles of gratitude he saw on the faces of the hundreds of impoverished Romanian orphans he helped meant much, much more to this most sensitive of souls.

It was in his native Northern Ireland that Joey Dunlop felt happiest, and that he chose to base his career at home brought him even more respect. (His one prolonged foray, racing in England for a season, away from his family and his tight circle of friends brought disenchantment.) The fact that he was allowed to return to the province and conduct his career from there says much about how he was regarded by his employer, Honda. His colleagues at the giant corporation saw a very particular gift and a very special spirit, which they knew could only flourish when surrounded by the people, the places and the things that had moulded him.

enjoyed a laugh, and if he appeared a little eccentric, he didn't mind being the reason for the laughter.

At the beginning of the year 2000, Joey's future was uncertain. He was forty-eight years old, but he knew he still had the 'bug' – the desire and the ability to keep winning. One day, Joey casually informed me that he was off to Australia the next morning. Why? 'I need a few weeks to get fit, and I'll get some peace out there.' It was then I knew: Joey would be back on his beloved Isle of Man

Shoulder to shoulder, Joey prepares to bump-start off the line with Mervyn Robinson at the 1975 Mid-Antrim 150.

With the bike sparkling in the rare Dundrogrough sunshine, Joey cranks his Yamsel into Tournagrough during the 350cc race at the 1976 Ulster Grand Prix.

that year. The offer of the very latest engineering miracle from Honda was the bait that hooked him. He'd decided that he was mentally and physically ready for the challenge, and I did not doubt his judgement for a second.

But I, like many others, was amazed by the events at the TT festival in June, a festival which is – and will surely remain – a celebration of Joey Dunlop. The versatility he'd shown all through his professional career was never more evident. He left his rivals trailing in his wake through Glen Hellen and beyond as he took the chequered flag on the state-of-the-art Honda SP1 'missile' to reclaim the Formula One crown, despite the challenges from the 'young lions'. He then climbed on board the two-stroke 250cc and 125cc bikes to win two more TT races before the week was out. The Millennium TT brought him three wins in total, and his overall record of twenty-six victories will probably never be surpassed. Typically, he'd once admitted to me that he had felt a little guilty a decade earlier when he overtook the late Mike Hailwood's record of wins because – unlike Joey – the Englishman no longer had the chance to extend his list of wins.

It has often been said that Joey never knew with just how much affection he was regarded. He seemed to wonder why anyone would be interested in watching him doing something he admitted was 'selfish'. But we knew why. It was the duty of people in my business to reflect the unique talent of the man and the

unconditional respect he commanded from his fans and from those who felt honoured to share a grid with him, his fellow racers.

I've been fortunate to know and to become friends with many sportspeople who have been at the top of their profession. Those friendships remain cherished. But in faraway Estonia, on 2 July 2000, the world of sport and I lost a unique friend. That he should have travelled to that country alone, after such sweet success at the TT, possibly to contemplate whether he could really give – or take – anything more to the sport, was again so typically unpredictable and extraordinary. But to Joey, such a trip was like calling in to a friend up the motorway from his home.

My memories of Joey are vivid. The public and private man were inseparable. He was at once the most complex and uncomplicated of people. Perhaps we tried too hard to explain his genius when his own simple understanding and unselfconscious ease with his talent would have been enough. In these pages are captured the moments of a very special life, one often lived in the spotlight. Yet Joey, the focus of attention, always seemed slightly detached from the glamour that accompanied his successes around the world. He was always his own man.

Joey Dunlop was indeed special, very special, and the 50,000 people who stilled a turbulent province in July 2000 to pay appropriate, but somehow inadequate, thanks for his life provided an image which hinted at that quality.

He was The King. I miss him.

Jackie Fullerton,
BBC Sport

Before joining Honda in 1981 and becoming their longest-serving rider, Joey had a brief liaison with the Suzuki firm. He was drafted in to help their Formula One world championship effort at Dundrod in 1980. Joey, racing under team orders to let Graeme Crosby finish in front, stormed into a massive lead at the Ulster Grand Prix before slowing and allowing his team-mate to pass him.

Alone with his thoughts, Joey sits on his stone-chipped 250cc Honda on the grid at the Ulster Grand Prix in 1995.

Joey Dunlop once said:
'I didn't want to be a superstar.
I just wanted to be myself. I hope
people remember me that way.'

I just wanted to photograph
Joey being Joey.

Stephen Davison, September 2000.

ting ready

Hair matted with sweat and still in leathers, Joey carries out some last-minute preparations on one of his machines. It would have been easy for a rider of Joey's standing to have had a team of white-gloved mechanics at his disposal, but he preferred to do the work himself – even in the middle of a race meeting. Unlike most other racers, Joey raced all kinds of machines. Aside from the pressures this placed on him as a racer, it also meant that his mechanical skills had to be of a very high order, especially as machinery became more complicated in recent times. Self-taught, his mechanical knowledge was encyclopaedic.

Joey's favourite race number, 3,
is put on the front of the fairing at a race meeting.
Although this number became associated with Joey, he
did not always race with it. It depended upon whether
or not it was allocated to him by the race organisers.
Six of his twenty-six TT wins were recorded when racing
under different numbers.

With little room to move, Joey changes a rear wheel at the North
West 200 in 1993. Unlike the Grand Prix circus, where riders hide away in
their motorhomes until the race is about to begin, there are no fenced-off
enclosures or restricted areas in Irish road race paddocks, allowing the
spectators to mix with the racers in the friendliest of atmospheres. Joey was
a permanent feature of this landscape, signing autographs or posing for
pictures with fans throughout the day.

With his tongue between his teeth and his face a mask of concentration, Joey makes some 'on the hoof' repairs to his 250cc Honda at the North West 200 in 1998. Work like this would often start in the most unlikely of circumstances, and before you knew what was happening an engine would be in pieces on the grass. Carburettor bowls and cylinder heads would lie in the gravel, and there would be dirt everywhere. As an uncle of mine once said, 'It's a wonder that the thing goes at all!' But eventually it would all go back together again almost as quickly, and Joey would wheel the bike onto the grid and win the race!

On almost every Saturday throughout the summer, Joey could be found in a race paddock at some small meeting in Ireland or further afield. These paddocks have always been family affairs, allowing young and old to watch their hero fettle his bikes. It was also a chance to chat with the man himself, as these youngsters in overalls did at the Carrowdore meeting in 1993.

Joey watches from the back of the race van as long-time helpers Andy Inglis and Willie Fulton prepare oil measures for the race bikes.

Any photographer or journalist who worked with Joey Dunlop will tell you that there were times when he was approachable and that there were times when he definitely was not. I discovered this for myself when I was sent to Joey's Ballymoney home in 1996 to get a picture of Joey with his wife, Linda, for a Sunday newspaper. Joey was in the shed, working away at the bikes, and only agreed to do the picture if I promised to be quick. I shot a few frames and began to leave. I had always wanted to photograph Joey at work in the shed, but it was obvious that this would not be a good time to ask. Nevertheless, the temptation of this once-off opportunity and the wonderful evening light streaming in through the back window were too great and I turned back in the yard. As I walked in through the shed door, the glare Joey gave me made it painfully obvious that I should not be there. Instead of asking for another shot, I pretended I was checking if I had left anything behind before beating a final, hasty retreat.

the

At any race meeting there was always a huddle of people around the back of Joey's van. The watching crowd would speak in whispers: 'He's changing the gearing', 'There's bother with the carbs' or 'She's off a cylinder'. Then a gap would open in the throng and you'd glimpse the hunched figure working in silence, hair hiding his face and tools scattered about the grass by his side. Making her ready to race.

paddock

Joey's race van was usually one of the last to arrive at the paddock. All the bikes were unloaded and made ready for scrutineering – the final, official check that bikes are raceworthy. They were then set out on stands, ready for last-minute adjustments and refuelling. Joey had several people in his team, such as sponsors and mechanics, who would help with these tasks and all the necessary paperwork. Almost everything took place in full public view and provided part of the fascination of watching a race. Sometimes it was almost as interesting standing in the paddock as it was watching the racing!

The rear window of the race van is used to store the famous number 3 plates at an Ulster road race meeting. Various legends have grown up around Joey's superstitions. He often wore a 'lucky' red shirt under his leathers, and if he couldn't have the number 3 he would have a number that was a multiple of three. He always dreaded the number 31 as this was the race number worn by fellow 'Armoy Armada' men Frank Kennedy and Mervyn Robinson when they were killed in race crashes. Joey had been worried about the year 2000 as he counted it his thirty-first season of racing.

Joey Dunlop on his way
to work! Tandragee 1994.

A Grand Prix Formula One motorhome this is not! Joey reflects on some finer detail of his race preparation in the spartan surroundings of his van. This is the van he used to travel the world to racing events and on his lone humanitarian missions to deprived areas in Eastern Europe. Helmets and paddock jackets share space with bottles of Mr Muscle domestic cleaner and the ever-present red toolbox. The race bikes were crammed in alongside one another at the end of the meeting.

On his aid trips to the orphanages of Romania and Albania, Joey would pack the van to the ceiling with supplies and set out alone, covering thousands of miles at the wheel and sleeping on board at night. But in spite of the anonymous vehicle, Joey was still recognised the world over. During one mercy mission, an uncooperative border-guard on a frozen Eastern European frontier was happy to let the Armoy man pass through – after he had proved he was indeed Joey Dunlop by showing his photograph in motorcycling magazines and signing an autograph or two.

Joey didn't have far to go for his tea at the Tandragee
race meeting – his race van sits side by side with the fish and chip cart in
the paddock. Generally these paddocks are fields donated for the day by a
local farmer. On a dry day everything is fine, but as the changeable Irish
weather turns to rain it is a very different story. It's not unusual to see
multi-thousand-pound Superbikes being rolled onto the grid with their
tyres covered in mud and grass, ensuring a cautious start to the race.

Two sets of Joey's leathers

hang on the back door of the race van at the Ulster Grand Prix meeting in 1995. The leathers had to be changed from race to race to match the colours of the different bike sponsors.

All eyes on the starter's flag. Joey lines up alongside Derek Young, Ian King and Alan Irwin at the Tandragee 100 meeting. Sadly, Ian King was killed at the Temple 100 in 1994; Derek Young and Alan Irwin retired several years ago. Because Joey's career spanned so many years he saw a lot of other racers come and go. This constant presence was one of the reasons he stayed in the public's affections for so long, and it also meant that in later years he was racing (and beating!) a whole new breed of rivals, some of whom were only half his age.

on
the
grid

A dead fly on the visor of his helmet comes in for some close scrutiny as Joey prepares to race. Flies and other insects are a major problem for road racers as they smash against the visor at over 100mph, making it difficult to see. Racers use 'tear-offs' on their visors, which they can peel away during the race. For Joey, cleaning the visor, like everything else, was carried out with meticulous care.

Joey's helmet was a very tight fit and required considerable effort to pull on. All of the Arai helmets he used were custom-made, with the internal foam shaped to suit his head. He almost always used the same hand-grip to pull the helmet down. North West 200, 1993.

Getting pushed off the line during a dull evening practice session at the North West 200 in 1997. The North West 200 was never one of Joey's favourite circuits after his fellow Armoy Armada pals, Frank Kennedy and Mervyn Robinson, were killed there in 1979 and 1980 respectively. Nevertheless, he won thirteen races on the course between 1979 and 1988.

Over the years the bikes would change, the colour of the leathers would vary, the hair would get shorter, but the one thing that remained the same was the famous yellow helmet. In earlier times the polycarbonate helmets had a joint running over the centre. To strengthen this vulnerable seam, Joey had stuck some black adhesive tape along the join, creating the trademark black band that ran across his yellow lid. He was Arai's longest-serving rider, having kept his distinctive helmet with the same brand since 1982.

Surrounded by dozens of revving engines and a mêlée of riders and officials, Joey retreats into a world of his own before the start of a wet day's racing at the Temple 100 in 1997. There were times when you could ask Joey to pose for a picture or give an interview, but this would not have been one of them! I always tried to choose my moments carefully if I had to ask for his cooperation for a picture, and I never found Joey anything other than courteous and obliging. The only stipulation he would make was: 'You'll

Quietly chatting with his sponsor, Andy McMenemy, on the grid at the North West 200 in 1999. Just a few days before he left for the final race meeting in Estonia, Joey learned of Andy's sudden death.

Still feeling the effects of his big crash at Brands Hatch the previous year, Joey lines up on the second row of the grid at the 1990 North West 200. The front row includes Joey's brother, Robert, on the 'works' Norton (12), Trevor Nation (5) and Carl Fogarty (4). Alongside Joey is Philip McCallen (2). After the accident, which left him with serious leg and wrist injuries, Joey was advised to give up the superbikes, but even at thirty-eight years of age he was still determined to battle back to fitness. Joey's physical and mental toughness are legendary, but perhaps the most important factor in motivating his comeback at this time was his love of motorcycle racing. By the end of the year he was winning again on the big bikes.

Gary Dynes (6), Joey Dunlop (3),
Denis McCullough (4), Owen McNally (1) and Ian Lougher
line up on the front row of the grid for the start of the
250cc race at the Ulster Grand Prix in 1999. Tragically,
Owen McNally died in a crash on the last lap of the
race. After Joey's death in July 2000, Gary Dynes was
killed and Denis McCullough seriously injured in a
crash at Glaslough, County Monaghan, in August 2000.

rs

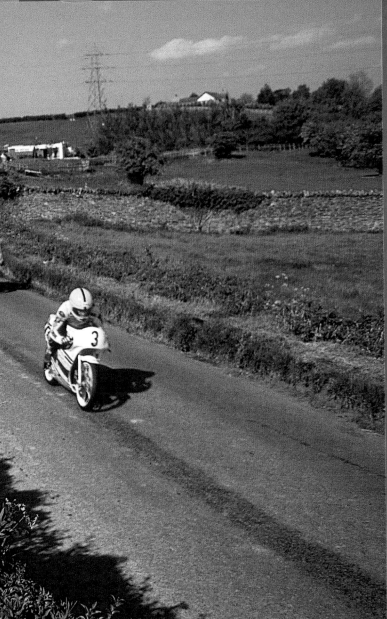

125cc racing

Joey leads Denis McCullough in the 125cc race at the Ulster Grand Prix in 1995. Up until his serious crash at Brands Hatch in 1989, Joey had never raced one of the 'tiddler' class bikes. But after the accident, the leg and wrist injuries he had sustained made it difficult for him to ride the bigger bikes and he turned his attention to the 125cc machines, becoming something of a specialist in later years. Indeed, it was on a 125cc bike, in 1993, that he beat Mike Hailwood's record number of fourteen TT wins.

Slipping the clutch with his left hand, Joey powers his 125cc Honda out of Church corner at the 1991 North West 200. Joey's approach to racing harked back to an earlier era in motorcycle sport. He raced machines of all sizes, types and capacities at every meeting. Four-strokes were mixed with two-strokes, the tiny 125cc engines with the massive 750cc machines. At the small Irish events there are only a few minutes between each race, which allowed Joey little time to adjust his style from one bike to another.

Robert Dunlop (1) chases brother Joey around Ballyboley corner at Carrowdore in 1993 on their 125cc machines. Throughout the 1990s most 125cc races on Ulster and Isle of Man roads involved close battles between the slightly built Dunlop brothers. Of the twelve Ultra-Lightweight (125cc) TT races held from 1989 to 2000, they triumphed in nine – Joey taking five wins and Robert taking four.

Pulling hard on the front brake, Joey is totally focussed as he flies into O'Hara's bends on his 125cc Honda at the Mid-Antrim 150 in 1998. This was Joey's 'home' course and he scored fifteen wins here. Although the races were always known as the Mid-Antrim 150, there had been many changes over the years. The '150' referred to the number of miles originally raced in the 1940s and 1950s when the main event of the day was a handicap race. In more recent years, the races were much shorter and the actual course was often altered or even moved to different roads altogether. But Joey was always versatile in his approach and so the wins kept coming in spite of the changes.

Although Joey was a very familiar figure to most racing fans, there was always an aura of mystery around him as well. Watching him before a race, I would try to glean an insight into what he was thinking or feeling. But he gave little away. There was always a sense of wonder as to what exactly it was that made him so special when he mounted a racing motorbike. It was part of the fascination of watching Joey Dunlop.

Joey on a Honda leads his brother, Robert, on a Norton at Metropole corner, Portrush, during the Superbike race at the 1991 North West 200. Eight years younger than big brother Joey, Robert's racing career as a 'works' rider at Norton was in the ascendant during this period. Joey, still battling his way back to full fitness after injury, had to play second fiddle to Robert, especially at the North West 200 where the younger Dunlop dominated in the early 1990s. Unfortunately, Robert also suffered serious injury in a TT crash, in 1994, robbing the fans of the spectacle of the brothers doing regular battle in the big bike classes.

Chatting with his brother Robert in the Villa Marina bar during the TT prize presentation in 1999. The brothers have shared many high and low points at the TT over the years, but perhaps their greatest adventure was their journey to the Isle of Man in 1985. They had decided to ferry themselves and their machines across the Irish Sea on a fishing boat. However, the boat struck heavy seas and the Dunlop brothers had to be rescued as it sank. Thankfully no one was hurt, and the bikes were eventually retrieved from the seabed. It is said that during the trip Joey had been busy frying chops in the galley when Robert asked if he had used enough salt. As the sea water came pouring in, Joey replied: 'I think there's enough now.'

Robert Dunlop, wearing his trademark hat, helps prepare brother Joey's Honda RC45 for the 1999 Ulster Grand Prix. Over the years the two brothers were rivals in many races, but off the track they worked closely together. This spirit of cooperation runs through the whole motorcycle racing fraternity in Ireland, with riders lending each other everything from tools to engines. Joey was well-known for providing assistance to other competitors. One veteran racer, Mick Chatterton, told how Joey quietly approached him at the start of TT 2000 and told him to call at the Honda garage. When he did, Joey gave him some engine parts. Such stories of 'Yer Maun's' generosity and sportsmanship are commonplace.

rivals

Chatting with Steve Hislop at Kirkistown in 1993. Eleven times TT winner, Steve Hislop was a Honda Britain team-mate of Joey's and a major rival at the big road race meetings. Throughout the 1990s, Honda continued to supply Joey with race bikes but the top machinery went to riders like Hislop, Carl Fogarty, Philip McCallen and Ian Simpson. Joey soldiered on, but as the decade drew to an end and some riders started to turn their backs on the TT, Honda came to rely once again on their longest-serving rider.

In the relaxed atmosphere of the
Carrowdore 100 paddock in 1993, Joey chats with fellow
racers Ian King, Raymond McCullough and John
McCullough. Throughout the 1970s, Joey battled with
Raymond McCullough for supremacy on the Ulster road
courses, and for many fans their dices provided the
best racing ever seen on these circuits. Intense rivals
on the track, they were firm friends off it; McCullough
was regarded as Joey's favourite road racer.

Joey shares a joke with David Jeffries on the podium at the 1999 Ulster Grand Prix at Dundrod. Joey had just beaten the seemingly invincible Jeffries in the Superbike race – the only time that the Yorkshireman had been beaten on the roads all season. Many people had begun to think that Jeffries was unbeatable, but once again the 'King' taught yet another 'Young Pretender' a lesson in pure speed.

250cc rac

Skimming the kerb at Ireland's bend on his beloved Dundrod course on the 250cc Honda in 1990. People would say that if you laid a penny on the road, Joey would pass over it every lap as he followed the same perfect line around the course.

ing

Leading Gary Dynes into Tournagrough at Dundrod in 1999, Joey keeps his eyes on the road ahead. Like Dynes, Joey was one of the last racers still riding these 250cc two-stroke machines. Increasingly, racing bikes are based on four-stroke production machines that can be bought in any dealership by road riders, but the two-stroke 125cc and 250cc machines are pure racing bikes, built only for competition. Forced to ride the production-based four-strokes in the bigger classes in recent years, it remained one of Joey's ambitions to race a Mick Doohan 500cc Grand Prix Honda at the TT: the purest form of factory racer in the world.

With the grass bending in his wake, Joey flies through the Dundrod bends on his 250cc Honda. An old man sitting on the bank beside me remarked, 'he would take the light from your eyes' – my favourite description of what it was like to witness Joey Dunlop in action.

Spectators line the grass banks of the Skerries course in County Dublin as Joey follows the verges. The Irish national road race meetings are held over narrow country lanes lined by trees and hedges. The road surface itself is often less than perfect, with the odd pothole or crack appearing. For Irish road racers this is all part and parcel of the nature of road racing, but for others, more used to racing on the purpose-built short circuits, the idea of racing on such roads is beyond comprehension. When Kenny Roberts, the American 500cc World Grand Prix Champion, was driven around the Temple course in County Down, he thought he was on a farm track and could not believe that these roads were used to race motorcycles. In the early 1980s, Virginio Ferrari, challenging Joey Dunlop for the World Formula One championship, arrived at the Dundrod course in County Antrim for practice. He did one lap and then went straight back to the airport, declaring that he would not race anywhere that had barbwire fences!

Long hair floating in the breeze, Joey steers his 250cc Honda through Quarry bends at Dundrod during Ulster Grand Prix practice. The practice sessions at races are invaluable for setting up the machines, but some of the machines Joey raced were notoriously difficult to get right. As a result, more testing was required. Stories about Joey taking bikes out for a run on the public roads near his home as he prepared for races are legendary. Working on the Honda SP1 before the 2000 North West 200, Joey decided to take the big bike for a blast on the Garryduff Road in front of his home. Unfortunately, he passed members of the local constabulary going the other way. Worried about the consequences should he be apprehended on a public road on a race bike, Joey sought refuge at a nearby house and rang home to arrange for a van to collect the bike and himself. Unknown to him, the police patrol had already stopped at his house. The sympathetic officers said they had not bothered to give chase because they wouldn't have been able to catch him, and they left Joey their best wishes for the races at the weekend!

Joey takes the wider line

through the hairpin bend during the 250cc race at Dundrod in the Ulster Grand Prix in 1997. Owen McNally (7), Ryan Farquarher (12) and James Courtney (5) kept to a tighter line.

Backmarker Andrew Marsden (22) looks like he's being pulled apart as Marc Fissette (36) and Joey make the final surge to the line in the 1997 250cc race at the Ulster Grand Prix. In one of the closest ever finishes in a motorcycle race in Ireland, Joey beat the Belgian by 0.03 of a second. Marsden, one lap behind, finished sixteenth.

This is what has become known as Joey's 'race face'. Commentators would ponder whether or not Joey 'had his race face on' when he came to the start-line. If he had, it meant that he would definitely be going all out for a win. He said himself that there were days when he knew he could win, and there were others when he knew it was better to let the race go. Perhaps the bike wasn't running properly or the weather conditions were unfavourable. Some days he just wasn't in the right frame of mind. It was never win or bust with Joey, but when he was determined to win there was no one who could deny him his victory.

changing

A reflective moment at the North West 200 in 1999.

faces

Racing across the water in England for one of the first times, a delighted twenty-four-year-old Joey poses for the camera at Oulton Park in Cheshire in 1976.

Keeping an eye on the opposition from the back of the race van. Whilst he may not always have looked as slick as some of the other race teams, Joey's approach to racing was professional and dedicated. Just how dedicated is illustrated by a story from his early years when he was racing with his brother, Jim. Jim and Joey had decided to practice the 'art' of falling off a motorcycle. The wide open sandy spaces of Portstewart strand were chosen as the softest landing place, and Jim proceeded to drive up and down the beach in a car with Joey perched on the bonnet. When Jim hit the brakes, Joey rolled off and curled up into a ball to protect himself. All was going well until Joey took the wheel and Jim tested his technique. Unfortunately, Jim found a harder patch of sand, breaking his collarbone in the process!

Sharing a joke with other riders in the warm-up area at the Tandragee 100, Joey was always willing to assist other aspiring racers with advice or practical help. Some years ago, a young racer hoping to improve his course knowledge asked if he could follow Joey around the TT course during early morning practice. Joey agreed, but after a while, as he concentrated more on the lap itself, he forgot about his young protégé. Trying to keep the rapidly disappearing yellow helmet in sight, the young racer approached the notorious Ballaugh Bridge far too quickly. He almost flew over the top of the Raven pub on the other side of the bridge, and quickly realised it would be better to let Joey go on without him!

Unlike many modern sportsmen, Joey was not overly concerned with his image. There were no designer shades or £100 haircuts from the trendiest salons in Belfast. He preferred to display his style on the race track, and even when fame and success came along he never changed. When I looked at Joey Dunlop, I saw a man just like the uncles who had taken me to see my first motorcycle races – they too were working men who rode bikes and were not scared to get their hands dirty. When Joey spoke, he talked with the same broad accent as ourselves. Can you imagine the pride we shared in watching one of our own take on the best in the world and win?

One of the best times to photograph Joey was just before the start of a race when he seemed to be in a world of his own, psyching himself up for the job in hand. At these times he appeared oblivious to all that was around him, so intense was his focus on the road ahead.

Sitting in the back of the race van, Joey enjoys a cigarette as he shelters from the rain at Dundrod in 1994. A lifelong smoker, Joey gave up the habit in 1996. Barry Sheene, another world champion motorcycle racer, recently told how Joey inspired him to stop smoking after they had met at a race meeting at Scarborough that year.

A relaxed Joey on the grid at the North West 200 in 1997. It was unusual to see Joey smiling before a race as he usually shut out everything around him and his face became a mask of concentration. Following Joey from the paddock to the grid was a thrilling experience, hearing the murmur of recognition pass through the crowd: 'There's Joey.' Fellow Honda racer Philip McCallen has told of the adulation Joey was greeted with when they raced as a team at the Suzuka Eight-Hour Race in Japan in the early nineties. As the pair of them walked to the pits, a stunned McCallen could only look on as the Ballymoney man was besieged by dozens of Japanese autograph hunters. It must have been difficult at times to go about his business knowing that all eyes were on him, but he appeared to be able to filter out every distraction when necessary.

Looking relaxed, Joey enjoys the evening sunshine at the North West 200 practice in 1999. In recent years he had been escaping the long Irish winters by taking a break in the heat of Australia. These trips allowed him to train and relax in peace for the new racing season. But even on the other side of the world, Joey could not escape recognition. He delighted in telling the story of how he was stopped for speeding by an Australian traffic cop whilst out for a spin on a road bike. 'Who do you think you are – Joey Dunlop?' asked the policeman as he spied the yellow helmet. Imagine his amazement when the Ballymoney man pulled off the helmet to reveal that he was indeed Joey Dunlop! No ticket was issued when Joey agreed to visit the station the next day to meet the rest of the motorbike-mad local police force.

the

Being small in stature, Joey had to be very fit to handle the big machines, such as the Honda RC30, that he specialised in racing. He can only just be seen on the bike as he hangs his weight to the inside while rounding York hairpin in the 1988 North West 200. As with most things, Joey had a pragmatic approach to keeping his fitness in check. Throughout the winter months he often worked as a steel erector with his two brothers, climbing ladders and clambering over girders rather than pumping iron at the gym.

big bikes

Joey keeps watch from the back of the pack as David Jeffries, Ian Duffus, Jason Griffiths and Adrian Archibald round Ireland's bend during the 600cc race at the 1999 Ulster Grand Prix at Dundrod. Especially in later years, Joey preferred to keep clear of the cut and thrust of tight battles on the road, shrewdly maintaining a distance. In this race his caution was justified – Jeffries brought down Duffus, causing Archibald to crash also. Unfortunately, Joey did not benefit from his astute manoeuvring as the race was stopped and the result declared from the positions of the previous lap.

Joey leads Jason Griffiths and James Courtney at Leathemstown corner during the 1997 Ulster Grand Prix. Joey is riding the 500cc Honda twin he had for that season. The bike was difficult to set up and had been temperamental in its performances. The home-made cardboard-and-duct tape affair at the front of the bike is a typical Joey-style attempt to solve an airflow problem. Such devices, put together in his Ballymoney shed, often proved as effective as the hi-tech parts supplied from Japan. He seemed to relish the challenge of working out these problems by himself. A commentator who visited Joey's workshop during the TT drew a compelling picture of a totally engrossed Joey working intently on his 125cc machine while his father, William, sat watching from the corner.

With the tyres barely making contact with the tarmac and his knee skimming the ground, Joey blasts his 750cc Honda RC45 through Quarry bends at the Ulster Grand Prix in 1999. V&M Yamaha's David Jeffries and Ian Duffus tried in vain to keep their faster 1,000cc machines in contention, but Joey maintained his lead to score perhaps his greatest ever win at Dundrod. As with his last ever lap of the Isle of Man course, his final lap speed of 125.146mph at the Ulster Grand Prix was his fastest ever. Few people imagined that he could beat the mighty David Jeffries on the all-conquering 1,000cc Yamaha R1, but Jeffries admitted after the race that he just could not keep up with the Ballymoney man.

Standing on the bank at Dundrod on a typically grey day in 1975, I heard, for the first time, the spine-tingling roar of racing bikes hurtling down the Deer's Leap before they broke into view under the trees at Cochranstown. This picture was taken at the spot where I watched that first race.

Joey on the Honda RC30 leads the Superbike pack into York corner in the Superbike race at the North West 200 in 1988. Pure road racing can be a cruel sport, four of the first six riders in this picture — Joey, Mark Farmer, Kenny Irons and Steve Henshaw — lost their lives whilst racing.

Totally focussed, Joey prepares to race at the 1995 Ulster Grand Prix.

With his head tucked behind the screen, Joey screams the Honda RC30 over Budore crossroads during the 1993 Ulster Grand Prix practice. On this stretch of the course the big bikes would be hitting over 150mph on roads lined with telegraph poles and concrete posts.

Leading the pack past the stone walls of Castle corner in the Superbike race at the 1990 Tandragee 100 meeting. The flag marshal, smoking a pipe and apparently oblivious to the speeding machine passing only inches from his feet, is holding a green flag, which indicates that the road is clear and it is safe to race. Any kind of danger and the flag would be changed to the yellow one, which he is also holding, to warn the riders to slow down. As the day wore on and the marshal's right arm began to tire, the flag drooped down until the riders were almost touching it with their heads as they passed by!

Joey wheelies the Shell Gemini Honda over the top of the awesome Deer's Leap Hill on the Dundrod course during the 1990 Killinchy 150 meeting. Farmers in cloth caps, with their sons and their grandsons, line the country hedges to watch the 'wee man' hurtle down the rollercoaster drop. Folk like himself, the spectators were astonished that one of their own could ride a motorbike so fast over roads they drove their tractors and cars on every other day of the year.

crash!

I only saw Joey Dunlop crash once. It happened at Castle corner, during the Tandragee 100 meeting, in 1999. Joey was leading the 125cc race from Owen McNally, Denis McCullough and Gary Dynes when the back wheel of his bike started to slide, throwing him over the handlebars and onto the road.

Thankfully, Joey was unhurt in this incident – unlike the bike, which needed some attention. The marshals provided a welcome soft drink as the 'inquest' began. It was the second year in a row that Joey had crashed while leading the 125cc race at this meeting.

after
the
race

In sweltering conditions at the Ulster Grand Prix in 1995, an exhausted Joey collapses onto the floor of his race van. Unlike top Grand Prix racers and Formula One drivers who only compete in one event per meeting, Joey was entered in four, five or even six races. Between races there was no plush, air-conditioned motorhome to relax in. But at forty-three years of age and having already won two races earlier in the day, Joey Dunlop pulled the leathers on again and returned to the track to score a third win in the blazing sunshine. It was this one hundred percent commitment that won him the hearts of so many people.

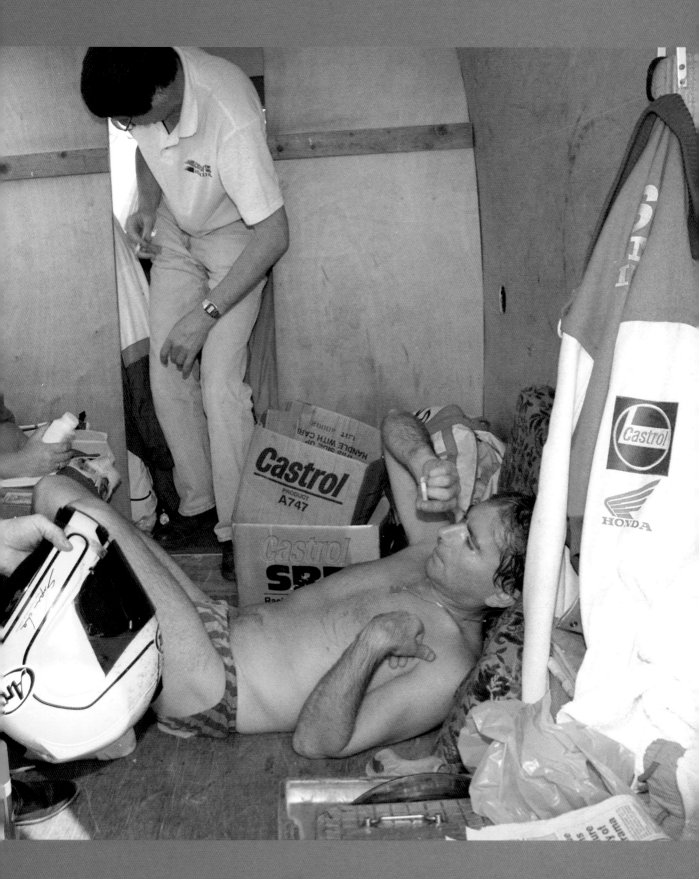

On a warm day and after hard racing (and winning) at the Carrowdore 100 meeting in 1993, Joey pulled off the leathers and sat down to a 'doorstep' sandwich and a mug of tea – from a Flintstones mug. As always, dozens of people were standing around the back of the van, but Joey remained unconcerned as he sat in his underpants enjoying his tea. As they say, there were no airs or graces with Joey Dunlop. I was disappointed to learn later that Joey did not like this photograph. It was not 'sneaked' – there were lots of people standing outside the van – and it was never my intention to belittle my hero. Joey did his job and I did mine. For me, this picture probably tells it as it was better than any other shot I ever took of Joey.

Before he gave up smoking several years ago, it was a post-race ritual for Joey to have a quick cigarette. Sometimes he only had enough time for a few quick puffs before the helmet was back on and the next race started. Ulster Grand Prix, 1995.

on the island

Ballaugh Bridge is one of the trickiest places on the Isle of Man course, a 'slow' 50mph humpback bridge approached flat out. Almost every rider has their own line and their own way of jumping over the bridge, but there was none more stylish than Joey Dunlop. Some of the showmen go for a big leap, but the landing can easily break a chain. Aware of this, Joey's approach was never too fast and he always managed to keep the front wheel in the air over the jump. This meant he landed on the back wheel – the best way to maintain machine control and get the power down on the road for the run through the village.

Joey at Rhencullen on the Honda RC45 during the 1999 Senior TT on the Isle of Man, one of the most spectacular places in the world to watch and photograph motorcycle racing. The silence is broken by the roar of the engines bouncing off the shops and houses in the narrow streets of Kirkmichael, before the bikes break into view at the petrol station. Fighting the bucking machines like rodeo cowboys, the racers wheelie past the 30mph sign on their back wheels – at over 130mph.

Brushing the railings at Ginger Hall on the 125cc Honda during Friday evening TT practice in 1998. Joey's racing line around the Isle of Man TT course was regarded by fellow competitors as the neatest and the fastest, but he had not always known it so well. When he first travelled to the TT races on the Isle of Man in 1976, he set off on his first lap not knowing which way the course went! He toured around to the Ballacraine Hotel corner and waited for the next rider so that he could follow him. As each of his 'guides' sped away, Joey waited for another to appear, eventually completing his first lap!

A Ballymoney man leads a Ballymoney man! Joey leads Adrian Archibald in the 1999 Junior TT at Creg Ny Baa. In recent years, Ulster racers have excelled at the Isle of Man TT races because of the experience they gain from racing on the road courses in Ireland – one of the last places in the world to have racing on closed public roads. The success of Joey Dunlop has provided an inspiration to many other racers, and the North Antrim area, with men like Dick and John Creith, Owen McNally, Donny Robinson and the Dunlop brothers, has produced more than its fair share of top men.

Ignoring the speed limits, Joey skims through Ballaspur on his 250cc Honda in the 1999 Lightweight TT. The TT course is 37.75 miles long around public roads used for ordinary transport during the rest of the year. Lined with walls, hedges, telegraph poles, road signs, kerbs and all the rest of the normal obstacles to be found on public roads, the course allows little margin for error. Changing from narrow village streets to tree-lined glens and then to open mountain moors, it offers a unique challenge and one that takes years to come to terms with. Smooth and fast, Joey Dunlop mastered this course like no other rider. In ninety-eight starts and twenty-six wins in twenty-five years he only crashed once, when petrol leaked on to his front wheel causing him to skid off at Sulby Bridge in 1986. He escaped unhurt.

With Ramsay shining in the sun in the background, Joey negotiates Guthries on his 250cc Honda during Friday evening TT practice in 1999. This is the road of which Joey was 'King': the TT mountain course. The mountain section winds for some sixteen miles over the top of Snaefell summit. There are no houses and few trees. On a bad day the fog and mist can drop in seconds, making this a bleak place to be stuck as a spectator or race marshal. But on a fine June evening it was a delight to stand on the banks and watch the yellow helmet sweep through the open curves, following the perfect racing line.

Feeling the pressure, Joey prepares for TT practice in 1998 following a crash at the Tandragee meeting a few weeks earlier, which had left him with a cracked pelvis, a broken collarbone, broken bones in his hand and only half of his wedding finger. In obvious pain, few would have given Joey much chance of adding to his TT wins tally, but he was once again to prove the pundits wrong with a brilliant win in the Lightweight event.

Keeping close to the kerb, Joey passes Bradden Church and the packed grandstand during the 1998 Ultra-Lightweight TT. Around 50,000 people go to the Isle of Man for the racing festival every June; Joey Dunlop was every fan's favourite. It was always a major asset for organisers of an event to be able to say that Joey Dunlop would be in the starting line-up. Joey loved to race and compete, even though he didn't always benefit in financial terms. Nevertheless, he was prepared to travel to meetings in far-flung places, such as Latvia and Estonia, where the promoters needed him a great deal more than he needed to be there.

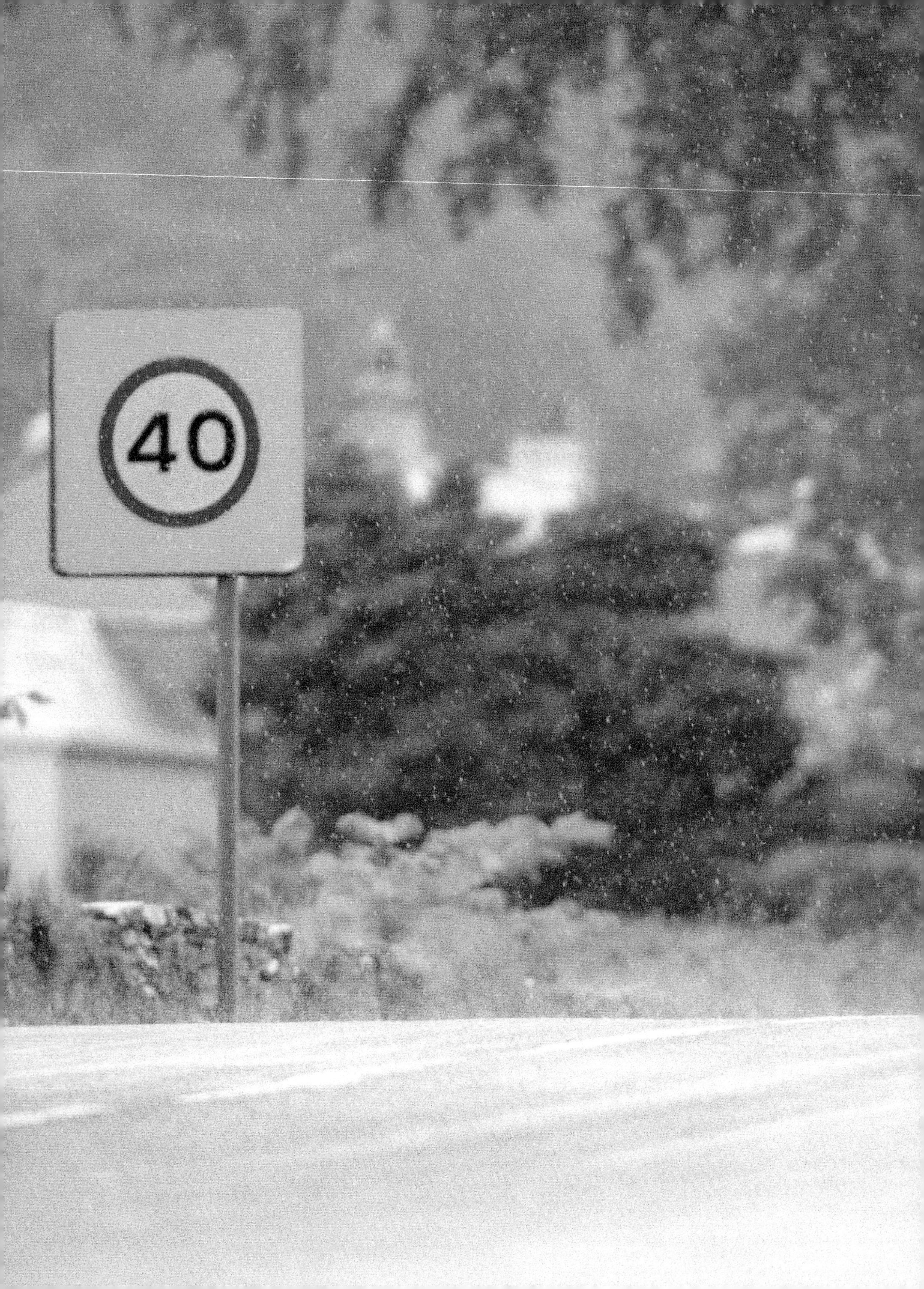
40

When Joey left the start-line on his 250cc Honda at the start of the 1998 Lightweight TT race, it was only spitting rain at the grandstand. By halfway around the first lap the skies had opened and torrential rain created treacherous conditions around the course. Aware of the worsening weather, the organisers had already decided to reduce the four lap race to three laps. The TT is one of the very few races where the bikes have to refuel to cover the race distance, and in this race most riders had chosen to come into the pits after the first lap. Normally in a three lap race this would have been the best strategy because the third circuit would have been a 'flying' lap, with no slowing down to enter or leave the pits. But Joey powered straight through the start and finish line after the first lap. Having seen similar conditions before, Joey had realised that the bad weather could lead to a further reduction in the number of laps. Shortly after he began his second lap, this was exactly what happened. Already some thirty seconds ahead, he now had an unassailable lead. Joey once again proved himself not just the fastest racer, but the best tactician around the TT course. As one observer remarked: 'As the race conditions changed, Joey moved from plan A to plan B, when the rest of the field had no plan at all.'

A fly for every mile: Joey's helmet after the Formula One TT in 1999.

For a photographer, covering the Isle of Man TT races is a dream and a nightmare all rolled into one. On the one hand, there are some vantage points, such as Creg Ny Baa or Guthries, which provide great photo opportunities. But on the other hand, there are few access roads to the 37.75-mile mountain course, making it very difficult to get back to the grandstand for the podium pictures. When Joey won the Lightweight TT on his 250cc Honda in 1998, I was taking pictures near Ramsay town and had planned to head back to Douglas after two laps for the celebrations. When the race was cut to two laps because of the bad weather, this plan was scuppered. By the time I got back to the grandstand, Joey had long since left the podium, but he was still doing interviews in his soaking wet leathers. He happily posed for pictures with his youngest daughter, Joanne, at the back of the van. The day was saved!

Joey enjoys an obviously popular victory in the 125cc race at the Tandragee 100 meeting in 1994. In total, he had more than 230 race wins at tracks all around the world. Regardless of the other names in the starting line-up, a Dunlop win has always been the biggest crowd-pleaser over the past twenty years and more. Men who would rarely display much emotion in normal circumstances were only too happy to wave a programme or shout unheard words of encouragement from the hedgerows as the yellow helmet whizzed past. If he won, it was the highlight of the day. If he lost, there were no recriminations because 'sure, he had nothing more to prove!'

champion

Sitting amongst a display of his racing trophies in Ballymoney in 1997, Joey holds the first trophy he ever won after finishing fifth on a 200cc Suzuki at the Mid-Antrim meeting in 1972. This remained one of his most cherished awards.

On a baking hot day in 1995, Joey won three races at the Ulster Grand Prix, scoring wins in both 250cc races and the Superbike race. The super-fast twists and turns of the Dundrod course, which was home to the Killinchy 150, the Dundrod 150 and the Ulster Grand Prix, made it one of Joey's favourite circuits. He stood on the top of the podium at Dundrod more times than any other rider: forty-eight times in total, with twenty-four wins in the Ulster Grand Prix, twenty-two in the Killinchy 150 and two at the Dundrod 150.

Another winner's cap and another winner's smile!

Almost unnoticed, Joey heads back to the van with another trophy for the sideboard after a victory at the Ulster Grand Prix. As he passed through the paddock quiet words of congratulations were offered and old-timers would come up to shake his hand, but there were no high-fives or whoops of joy, no hugging or kissing or back-clapping. Modest and unassuming, Joey never made a big scene after his wins. In earlier years, the announcer would call in vain for Joey to come to the podium to bask in his moment of glory. But Joey could never be found – almost inevitably there would be another bike to make ready for the next race.

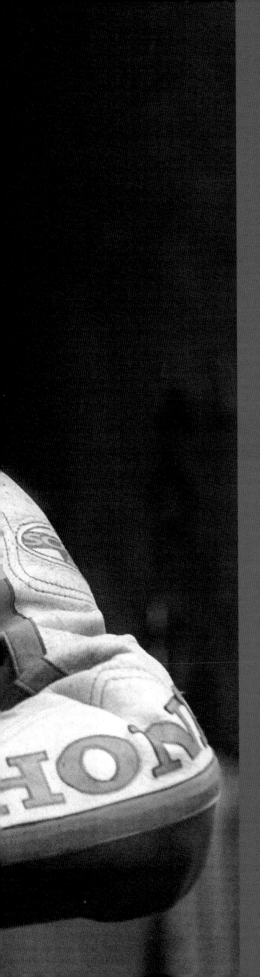

the final lap

The Cookstown 100 meeting in April is traditionally the first Irish road race of the season. In 2000, the Friday evening practice session was held in glorious sunshine, but by Saturday morning the heavens had opened and it poured with rain throughout the races. It was a big day for Joey as it was his first run on the roads on the new Honda SP1 twin, which he was to race at the TT in June. In spite of his problems, which included a crash whilst leading the 250cc race, Joey was in good spirits. He kept a bright yellow towel on hand to dry off after each race.

At the start of the 2000 season, Joey was introduced to the new Honda SP1 bike at the Ulster Motorcycle Show. This new Honda road machine was to form the basis for his race bike later in the season. Joey was also presented with his old RC45 race bike by Bob McMillan, General Manager of Honda. It was suspended from the ceiling of his bar in Ballymoney as an attraction for visitors. But as Honda struggled to make their machines competitive in the early part of

the 2000 season, Joey threatened to bring the RC45 out of retirement. With the addition of the 'works' engine from Aaron Slight's World Superbike racer, the new SP1 satisfied Joey's demands for more power and the threat was lifted. However, the tale did not end there. Remarkably, Joey took the RC45 down from the ceiling and loaded it into the van bound for the ill-fated meeting in Estonia in July 2000. Riding it the day before his fatal crash, he scored a brilliant win.

A study in concentration on the 250cc Honda on the Coast Road at the North West 200 in 2000.

Joey's final Irish road race podium after he won the 125cc race at the Tandragee 100 in May 2000. Sharing the podium are Darren Lindsay (centre), second in the race, and third-placed Denis McCullough. Also present is David Wood, formerly Joey's manager, representing the race sponsors. The day had started controversially when the riders refused to race because of a new chicane that had been added to the course as part of a safety drive introduced by the Motor Cycle Union of Ireland (MCUI) for the year 2000. Joey had been one of the first riders to pack his bikes back into his van. But after prolonged debate, the riders took to the grid and, as always, Joey had the situation weighed up. He blasted into the lead from the start, realising that the chicane would force the following riders to queue up in order to pass through the narrow gap. Building up a substantial lead early on, he eased off towards the end for an easy win.

For the last couple of seasons there was a new addition to Joey's wardrobe: spectacles. He needed them for the close work on his bikes, but he was not that keen to be photographed wearing them. He was carrying out some work on the carburettor of his 125cc Honda at Aghadowey in April 2000 when this picture was taken. Later, the spectacles were returned to their storage space — in the toolbox!

The strain is obvious as Joey focusses on the task of winning the Formula One TT in 2000 on the special Honda SP1. Honda were beaten in the Formula One race for the first time ever in 1999, when Joey, hampered by a wheel change on the Honda RC45, trailed in second to David Jeffries on the Yamaha R1. However, Honda showed faith in their longest-serving rider by giving him the 'works' SP1 machine for TT 2000. The pressure was back on the forty-eight-year-old Dunlop. As Joey said, the look on the Japanese mechanic's face betrayed the question: why are we giving our best bike to this old man? But Joey was to reward the firm's belief in him.

With his knee only inches from the kerb, Joey rounds Quarterbridge on the Honda SP1 on the third lap of his epic Formula One TT race at TT 2000. Setting a blistering early pace on damp roads, Joey built a lead that proved unbeatable. Twenty years after first racing a Honda, Joey gave the Japanese factory perhaps their most memorable victory in the Isle of Man. Incredibly, Joey spurned formal contracts with the company. As Honda race boss Neil Tuxworth put it, 'he never signed a contract because everyone knew his handshake meant more.' Everyone present that day knew they were witnessing a remarkable piece of motorcycle road racing history.

Joey enjoying a TT tradition – a pint for the winning rider in the press centre after his Formula One victory at TT 2000. Over the years, Joey would have supped twenty-six of these as he waited to be interviewed by the world's media following his wins in the Isle of Man. Most TT journalists have been covering the event for years and were familiar figures if not friends. Joey moved among them, quietly answering questions in one-to-one interviews – a very different atmosphere from the cut-throat press conferences that follow Grand Prix races. And there was always time for a few more pints in the beer tent afterwards with fellow riders and friends.

Kate Hoey, the County Antrim-born UK Minister for Sport, congratulates Joey after his Formula One win at TT 2000. Completely caught up in the joy of the moment, Ms Hoey went on to present Joey with the winner's garland on the rostrum. A humble man by nature, Joey always appeared slightly bashful when he discovered that these VIPs were only too delighted to have the chance to meet him.

Beaming with pleasure, Joey enjoys a well-earned drink in the winners' enclosure after the TT 2000 Formula One race. Initially, he seemed tired and weary after two hours and 226 miles of racing, but as the minutes passed he relaxed and began to relish the crowd's obvious delight in his historic win.

Joey prepares to spray the champagne from the TT 2000 Formula One podium. Unfortunately, he didn't actually manage to pop the cork because he dropped the wet bottle. The strain of holding the heavy Honda SP1 over the bumps and jumps of the Isle of Man roads had weakened his grip. The wet bottle, made slippery from the champagne Joey was doused with by Michael Rutter and John McGuinness, slipped from his grasp.

Summerland, TT 2000, and a selection of Joey's TT replica trophies are on display at an exhibition celebrating his career. Joey started in ninety-eight TT races and won twenty-six of them; the first win was the Jubilee race in 1977 and the last was the Ultra-Lightweight (125cc) race in 2000. The winner and the finishers within a given percentage of the winner's time receive silver or bronze replicas of the winged Mercury trophy. Joey won eighty replicas in total.

Aside from his thousands of trophies, Joey collected a vast array of other racing memorabilia. Leathers, helmets, boots, gloves, knee sliders, diplomas and photographs joined his bikes and silverware at a special exhibition in the Isle of Man in 2000, which celebrated his twenty-fifth year of racing at the TT. Most of these items were usually stored in an attic above the shed at his Ballymoney home.

When I spotted this road sign near Ballaugh village as I was driving around the TT course during TT practice week, I knew it could make a special picture of Joey Dunlop. In 1988, Joey had joked that he felt he was getting too old for the racing in the Isle of Man and by 2000, at forty-eight years of age, a lot of people were saying that he was past it. His Formula One victory on the opening Saturday of TT 2000 proved the critics wrong, and I felt sure he would add to his tally of wins in the Lightweight race on his 250cc Honda on Monday. I arrived early at my chosen spot, but the race was delayed for several hours because of mist on the mountain section. Everywhere was soaking wet so I couldn't sit down on the bank, but I didn't want to walk back into the village as a lot of other photographers would be there. As a breed, photographers like to keep an eye on each other and I didn't want anyone following me back out to the sign to 'share' my picture. So I stood on my own in the miserable rain for nearly four hours – then it was all over in a split second as Joey flashed by. His age was probably the last thing on his mind! For me, the main worry was whether or not the picture was sharp as I sprinted along a disused railway line to start the twenty-mile drive back to the grandstand to cover his celebrations on the winners' rostrum!

Joey sprays the crowd with champagne after winning the Lightweight 250cc race at TT 2000. Before the race, he had told a reporter that he would be taking it easy after his exertions on the big bike in the Formula One event. When reminded of this in the winners' enclosure, Joey declared: 'I was taking it easy!'

A delighted Joey salutes the crowd from the top of the podium after scoring the second of his TT victories in the Lightweight race in the Isle of Man in 2000.

After scoring three TT wins in a week and bringing his total tally to twenty-six wins in twenty-five years, the Isle of Man government felt they should mark Joey's achievements in a special way during the final prize presentation of TT 2000. Minister for Tourism David Cretney presented him with the Isle of Man's Sword of State, mounted on a wooden plinth. Geoff Cannell, the TT commentator, immediately saw a unique photo opportunity. Pulling the sword off the plinth, he handed it back to Mr Cretney and motioned for Joey to get down on his knees to be 'knighted'. An overwhelmed Joey was declared 'Sir Joey Dunlop' in front of his delighted family, friends and fans.

Holding aloft the famous winged Mercury trophy, Joey poses for pictures at the final TT 2000 prize presentation in Summerland. Having received his haul of silverware and taken the plaudits of the crowd, Joey returned to the public bar with everyone else, simply one of the boys enjoying the *craic*.

Honda Britain's General Manager, Bob McMillan, shares a joke with Joey during the final prize presentation of TT 2000 at Summerland. McMillan was asking the crowd if they thought Joey should come back to the TT for another year and, of course, the fans roared their approval that he should. The question of Joey's retirement had been raised and dismissed many times over the years. A few weeks before this year's TT he said, 'I hear rumours all the time that I'm going to retire, but the truth is I don't know when I'm going to call it a day.'

On his way to winning his last TT race, Joey skirts the railings at Bradden Bridge on his 125cc Honda during the Ultra-Lightweight race at TT 2000.

Urged on by the fans, Joey negotiates Bradden Bridge during the Ultra-Lightweight TT at TT 2000. Whilst he was always the fans' favourite, Joey would rarely acknowledge his supporters while he was racing. There was no waving, no matter how far he was in the lead, and he would never celebrate race wins with wheelies or burn-outs like so many other racers. An understated 'Aye, it was alright!' was his usual response when confronted by admiring fans and media as he pulled off his helmet after winning a race.

Joey referees as Denis McCullough and Robert Dunlop spray each other with champagne on the podium after the Ultra-Lightweight TT 125cc race at TT 2000. This was Joey's third win of the week and his last Isle of Man victory. McCullough came in second and brother Robert, third. Joey was taking part in the 600cc race later in the day, so he didn't open his own bottle of champagne.

Joey shakes hands with David Jeffries in the winners' enclosure after the Senior TT in 2000. Jeffries won the race, breaking the 125mph lap speed for the first time in the process. Jeffries's V&M Yamaha team were ecstatic after the win, and Joey, although obviously disappointed at finishing third, was one of the first to congratulate the young Yorkshireman on his success. Joey's final lap of the race, at 123.87mph, was his quickest ever around the Isle of Man course.

After winning the Ultra-Lightweight 125cc TT earlier in the day, Joey rode the Harris 600cc Honda in the Junior TT on the Wednesday of TT 2000 race week. His win tally was three for the week so far, but that wasn't the end of it. He flew through these trees and bends on the approach to the Gooseneck to take a fourth place on the 600cc machine. Finally, he emerged on the Honda SP1 for a Senior TT practice run – a total of nine laps and almost 340 miles in one day over the toughest race course in the world.

The Isle of Man scouts work throughout TT race week on the massive manual leaderboard at the Glencrutchery Road grandstand. It has become something of a TT tradition that the winner of the Senior TT is asked to sign autographs and meet the tireless young workers. In 2000, the scoutmaster asked Joey, rather than race-winner David Jeffries, to meet the youngsters. As everyone else in the pits began to pack up after the two-week festival, Joey crossed the road to sit amongst the children, happily signing his name and posing for pictures. This was the last photograph I ever took of Joey Dunlop.

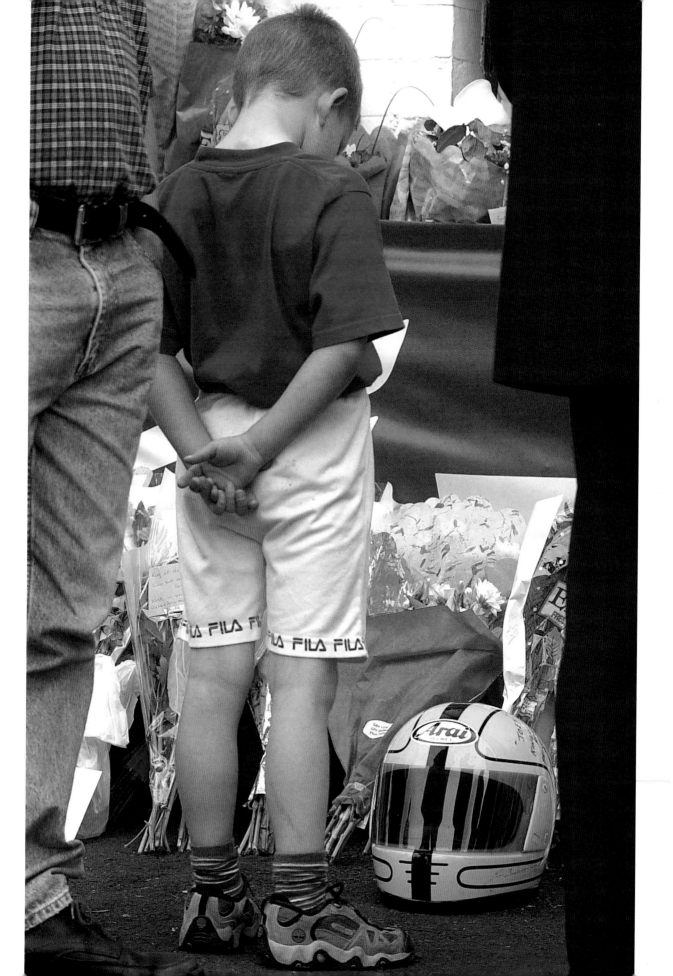

A respectful youngster outside Joey's Ballymoney bar reads the message on a Joey Dunlop replica helmet, left as a mark of respect by a fan. Offering a place where people could come to pay tribute, the bar became a shrine as fans travelled to County Antrim from all over Ireland to leave flowers and sign the books of condolence in the town.

Joey lost his life in a race meeting in Estonia on Sunday, July 2 2000. He was killed instantly when his 125cc Honda skidded off the track in pouring rain and hit a tree. He was lying in second place in the race, having already won two races earlier in the meeting. Stunned by the news, the people of Northern Ireland struggled to find a response. A simple floral tribute, one of the first left outside Joey's bar in Ballymoney, encapsulated the feelings of so many.

It is estimated that some 50,000 people attended Joey Dunlop's funeral on Friday, July 7 2000. Only from the air was it possible to appreciate the immense scale of the crowd. People travelled from all over the world to the small County Antrim town of Ballymoney to pay their respects to the 'People's Champion'. As *Motor Cycle News* wrote: 'There has seldom been a motorcyclist with whom the word legendary sits so easily.'

Joey's funeral cortège makes it way to his final resting place at Garryduff Presbyterian Church, Ballymoney, little more than a mile from his home. A massive crowd gathered at Joey's house and the route along the quiet country road was lined with mourners who fell in behind the procession as it passed. The only sounds on Joey's last journey were the low drone of the engine of the funeral hearse and the footfalls of the people walking behind it.

IN LOVING MEMORY OF
JOEY DUNLOP O.B.E., M.B.E.
WINNER OF 26 T.T. RACES (1977-2000)
"KING OF THE MOUNTAIN"
WHO DIED WHILST RACING IN ESTONIA,
2ND JULY 2000.
FROM THE GOVERNMENT AND PEOPLE
OF THE ISLE OF MAN
AND ALL HIS FANS WORLDWIDE.

M.R.M. SMITH Aug 2000

During the Isle of Man tribute to Joey, this plaque was unveiled by his wife, Linda, at the start and finish line on the TT course. It stands as a mark of honour to one of the TT's greatest sons.

Following his death, the Isle of Man government arranged a tribute to Joey Dunlop for August 27 2000. This included a lap of honour in his memory around the TT circuit. Over 10,000 bikers took part, forming a line over seventeen miles long. The course was lined by many thousands more Manx residents, who loudly applauded the riders and ensured Joey was appropriately honoured.

'We will never see his like again.'

Joey Dunlop, 1952–2000